PROJECT DELIVERY

VOLUME I   ISSUE 2   MAY 1999

SHIVE-HATTERY   **INFORMATION ON PROJECT MANAGEMENT, DESIGNER-LED DESIGN-BUILD AND OTHER PROJECT DELIVERY ISSUES**

LESSONS FROM ONE OF THE MOST QUOTED PEOPLE IN THE WORLD!

IF YOGI BERRA WERE A PROJECT MANAGER, HE WOULD SAY...

Dale Moore

INSIDE:

FOR MORE INFORMATION OR SUGGESTIONS CONTACT:

DALE MOORE
CORPORATE OFFICE
OPX 170
319.362.0313
INTERNAL E-MAIL

Those of you who have visited my space at the Corporate office may have noticed my copy of *The Yogi Book* placed right along side my business and project management books. Yogi is priceless. When I need a lift, I often read a few quotes from *The Yogi Book*. I get a few laughs and instantly feel better.

The truth is we can learn valuable lessons about project management from many of Yogi's famous quotes. Now, the key to Yogi-isms is Yogi's simple logic. He may take a different avenue than you or I would to say what he wants to say, but it's the fastest, truest route. Here are my thoughts on what we can learn about project management from a few of Yogi's more famous quotes.

"It ain't over 'til it's over!"

Project management is guiding a project from beginning to end. Creating a good project plan and negotiating a good professional services agreement are essential, but in themselves will not assure the delivery of a good project. Well-planned projects that have poor communications and are not guided, monitored and controlled consistently will certainly experience less success for all stakeholders than they potentially could.

Projects are filled with uncertainty and changes. It is essential that project managers identify and manage uncertainties and changes from the beginning to the end of the project. This is why we need a core group of professional project managers whose job it is to guide our multi-discipline and medium and larger size projects.

"You've got to be careful if you don't know where you're going 'cause you might not get there!"

Projects that are not well planned have a greater chance of failure than those that are planned. Yes, it is possible to muddle through by use of brut force and talent and end up with a reasonably successful project. We do this — far too often. But think how much more successful those projects could be and how much more fun it could be to work on these projects if they were properly planned — if we knew where we were going and how we are going to get there.

"When you come to the fork in the road, take it!"

Throughout the course of a typical project, situations will call for the project manager to make numerous decisions. The project manager will often be faced with the need to make a .... information. ...... balance and

ued on back

D1449818

BEST PRACTICES

THIS COLUMN IS INTENDED TO SHARE SOME BEST PRACTICES THAT WE HAVE SEEN AROUND THE COMPANY OR HAVE LEARNED FROM OUTSIDE SOURCES. SCOTT BRALEY, AIA AND PROJECT MANAGEMENT CONSULTANT TO THE A/E INDUSTRY, DEFINES BEST PRACTICE AS THOSE ACTIONS THE FIRM TAKES TO GET THE BEST RESULTS IN THE INDUSTRY. SO PARAPHRASING BRALEY, THIS COLUMN IS ABOUT THOSE ACTIONS INDIVIDUALS ARE TAKING TO GET THE BEST RESULTS IN THE FIRM. OUR GOAL IS FOR THESE PRACTICES TO BECOME THE BEST IN THE INDUSTRY. –DEM

Plan to Replan and Replan Kevin Trom, project manager for the local government team in Iowa City and member of the PM leadership class, has taken the Scott Braley advice we offered in the April newsletter to a new level. Kevin prepares an initial project plan with his team and then actively updates the plan with his team every two weeks. Kevin says this has improved his results and his team members like it!

Project Manager Notebooks The Iowa City office has developed a standard project manager's notebook. The tabbed notebook is prepared by the office support team. It contains project management sections with project management process forms and project documentation sections. Project managers request the notebook for those jobs where it is an appropriate tool. Iowa City PMs report this saves them significant setup time and gets the documentation process off to a good start. Clients have also commented on how professional we look when they see the notebooks at meetings. *This is an idea all offices could easily copy! Contact Carrie Canning in Iowa City for more information.*

SUBMIT YOUR BEST PRACTICE TO DALE MOORE FOR FUTURE ISSUES OF PROJECT DELIVERY.

Project Tracking Technique Ken Raiche, full time project manager on the industrial team in the Cedar Rapids office, has developed a method to successfully track projects. At appropriate intervals for each project, Ken asks each team member to estimate the time required to complete their respective assigned activities. This, in effect, provides percent complete information to compare against actual cost. The estimate to complete information is gathered by electronic budgeting spreadsheets that each team member completes. The information is then compiled by linking all sheets to an electronic summary sheet. Ken reports this is working well, but requires team member training and trust building. *Call Ken Raiche in Cedar Rapids for more details.*

Typical Project Plan Outlines The Des Moines office has developed typical outlines for project plans of various sizes. *Another idea that can easily be stolen. Contact Russ Schroeder or Jim Wignall in Des Moines for more information.*

Small Projects Management Plan The Moline office has developed a standard five-step plan for managing small projects. These are projects that are typically performed by one or two people of the same discipline who are often not the project manager. Craig Sorensen, project manager on the CII team in Moline and member of the PM leadership class, defines the five managing steps as follows:

• The project manager makes sure the right person is performing the work.
• The project manager reviews the proposal/contract. This is the project plan. 10 to 15 percent of the budget is allowed for project management.
• The performing team member must notify the project manager when work begins.
• The project manager and team member must discuss schedule and risks.
• The project manager is involved in the invoicing and closeout.

Contact Craig Sorensen in Moline for more details.

Divide Desired Project Results into Three Categories Jim Lewis, President of the Lewis Institute and author of Project Planning, Scheduling and Controlling, suggests that project managers look at the desired results of their project and divide them into three categories as the work begins — the "musts", the "wants", and the "nice-to-haves". Lewis suggests immediately burning the "nice-to-haves" and spending all of your time on the other two categories with the greatest priority given to the "musts" category.

ARE WE LEARNING FROM PAST PROJECTS?

Dale Moore

What must we do to learn from our past projects?

In an article printed in the March 1999 issue of *PM Network*, Neal Whitten, president of the Whitten Group, project management consultants and trainers, suggested that firms and organizations must practice two things before we can really learn from our past project experiences. First, we must perform post-project reviews when a project or a major phase of a lengthy project is completed. Second, we must apply the lessons from our previous projects to our new project plans. He also advocates that project managers prove to management that they have done this.

How are we doing? We have a process to do the first part. It is the responsibility of every project manager to follow the process. I trust you are using it. But how are we doing on the second part? Perhaps there are two parts to this question. First, project managers must routinely incorporate past learning into project plans. Second, project managers and teams need to know the lessons learned from other projects, throughout the entire organization.

The Des Moines office creates a lessons learned task force.

The Des Moines office has created a task force to address this issue. The task force includes Bob Bisenius, Anne Cameron and Russ Schroeder. They have just started their work. We intend to share the results of this work with the entire company, so that we can get much closer to the type of practice Neal Whitten described. Thanks to Bob, Anne and Russ for taking on this challenge! Stay tuned for updates!

Observation from a post project analysis.

I recently ran across a copy of a post project analysis summary in my file that was prepared last summer. Greg Gerdes and the Bloomington office building team prepared the summary for a project they performed for another office. The team identified 19 problems, the most likely root cause of each and what they could have been done to avoid or minimize the problem. The results are revealing. Here is a summary:

Nine problems were caused by process related issues and could have been avoided by better use of processes, several being related to project planning processes.

Six problems were caused by communications-related issues.

Two problems could have been avoided by more experience on the team.

Two problems were not completely diagnosed.

Of the 19 problems, the team said at least 15 were directly related to poor use of project management processes and communications. Recall the excerpts from the John Simonds article that appeared in the April issue of *Project Delivery*. Simonds said the top two practices of highly successfully project managers were 1) a focus on communications and 2) a commitment to project planning processes.

I suggest the above correlation is not a coincidence. We can all learn these lessons today. Commit to practicing and improving project communications and project planning! You will be more successful! ▲

fact: For the first quarter of 1999, the overall Shive-Hattery project variance is minus 0.5%. This performance is consistent throughout the company and represents some of the best overall performance we have seen — or at least for as long as this author can remember. The question? Have we really turned the corner?

> "THE MASTERS DEGREE IN PROJECT MANAGEMENT IS EXPERIENCE!"
> – JIM WANSACK

> "THERE IS A DIFFERENCE BETWEEN FOUR YEARS OF EXPERIENCE
> AND ONE YEAR OF EXPERIENCE FOUR TIMES."
> – DALE MOORE

Alice said, "Would you tell me, please, which way I ought to go from here?"
"That depends a good deal on where you want to get to", said the Cat.
"I don't know where - - - ", said Alice.
"Then it doesn't matter which way you go", said the Cat.
from *Alice's Adventures in Wonderland* by Lewis Carroll

Don't plan in more detail than you can manage. Keep project management as simple as possible.

LESSONS
continued from front cover

judge the benefit of waiting to obtain more information versus moving forward with the best decision that can be made with the available information. Procrastinating and not selecting a route when we come to the "fork in the road" is not acceptable and can be disastrous. Project managers who master the art of risk taking by quickly accessing the reality of the situation and making the best decision with available information will be more successful than those who do not. Project managers will also have to determine those times when decisions must be delayed in favor of gaining additional information or a client's decision. Again, we need professional project managers who are focused on the role of project management and can recognize and make those crucial decisions in a timely manner.

"We made too many wrong mistakes!"

Yogi actually said this after losing the 1960 World Series to the Pittsburgh Pirates. A series the Yankees should have won. Yogi realized teams make mistakes, but recognized the Yankees did not learn or recover from those little mistakes as the series progressed. The same is true for project management. We know there are uncertainties and mistakes will be made. However, we must be alert to those mistakes and make adjustments as the project progresses. Otherwise, the little mistakes will escalate into more significant problems.

It's d'eja vu all over again!"

How many times have we experienced the same mistakes on projects over and over? (I am beginning to sound like Yogi.) The answer, of course, is to learn from our mistakes

and to change our processes so past mistakes are not repeated. This is why we need professional project managers who will conduct post project reviews and capture lessons learned.

"It ain't over 'til it's over!"

This quote is so good it is worth a second look. Good project managers are good closers — period! Let's face it. Some project managers are having difficulty getting projects filed, getting the EIS

TOOLS AND TIPS

SUBMIT YOUR TOOL TIPS TO DALE MOORE FOR FUTURE ISSUES OF PROJECT DELIVERY.

Use the Power of the Work Breakdown Structure (WBS) – The WBS is a powerful tool that looks simple, but yet is underutilized and often overlooked by project managers. Use the WBS to separate your project into various components, or levels. The first level is the project name. Continue to breakdown your project to deliverables (nouns) and finally to individual tasks or activities (verbs). Don't break the project down any further than necessary. Activities usually occur at levels three, four or five. Dr. James Taylor, PMP, consultant, teacher and writer, says, "The WBS is perhaps the most useful project management tool. When used correctly, WBS is the basis for planning, scheduling, budgeting and controlling the work of the project."

Input Deliverables and Activities into MSP in WBS Format – The "indent" and "out-dent" feature of MS Project make it easy to input project deliverables and activities in WBS format. I highly recommend the WBS format. It makes your Gantt chart easier to read and follows normally accepted practices of project management.

Critical Tools makes WBS use easy – Critical Tools is a great "tool". I hope you are beginning to use it. You can create a "chart" version of your WBS by two simple clicks. (First, click the WBS icon while in MSP. Then, click on "template.wbt".) Your WBS in MSP will convert to a nice useful chart. You ask, "Can I start with the chart view". Yes, you can! Critical Tools allows you to click on a blank WBS screen and drag down. A box will form. Next — click and drag down on the first box. Another box will form and so on. You can enter information (like activity name) into the boxes by simply clicking on the center area of the box. A dialogue box will appear allowing you to input such information as the name of the activity. Call Dale Moore if you need help getting started.

Try the Leveling Gantt View – In MSP, try the Leveling Gantt view. Go "Views", then "More Views" and then "Leveling Gantt". This view provides an excellent way to see the critical path and the amount of float in non-critical tasks without going to the PERT view.

completed, sending out client and team member surveys and completing post project reviews. This should be the easy part of the project — a time to celebrate. Professional project managers will develop the discipline and processes to make project closeout an easy and enjoyable activity. ▲

Yogi Berra played for the New York Yankees from 1947 to 1963. He played in a record 14 World Series during that time and was the American League's most valuable player three seasons.

The Yogi Book by Yogi Berra is published by Workman Publishing Company, 1998, ISBN 0-7611-1090-9

PROJECT DELIVERY

VOLUME I   ISSUE 4

JULY 1999

SHIVE·HATTERY

INFORMATION ON PROJECT MANAGEMENT, DESIGNER-LED DESIGN-BUILD AND OTHER PROJECT DELIVERY ISSUES

WE ARE IN A RISKY BUSINESS!!

ALLOCATING RISKS FAIRLY AMONG THE STAKEHOLDERS IS THE KEY

Dale Moore

INSIDE:

FOR MORE INFORMATION OR SUGGESTIONS CONTACT:

DALE MOORE CORPORATE OFFICE OPX 170 319.362.0313 INTERNAL E-MAIL

Every time we enter into a contract with a client, whether written or unwritten, we are taking on risk. You might say we are in a risky business. How much risk do we take? Right frankly the answer to that question requires good business judgment and experience. Project leaders must develop the appropriate judgment. Here are some thoughts that will help you.

The first thing to understand about project risk is that *all stakeholders* must accept risks - not just the design professional. Stakeholders for a design and construction project usually include the client, the contractor(s) and the design professionals. In certain circumstances, the stakeholders may also include parties like developers and end users.

How much risk should each stakeholder take on? A good "rule of thumb" is to allocate the risk in proportion to the potential rewards from the project. Remember that the design professional's potential rewards are usually much less than those of the contractor or the owner.

How much risk should we take on? Obviously this will vary from project to project. I offer the following four simple rules to use when determining how much risk to accept for Shive-Hattery or Shive-Hattery Construction.

1. Don't accept risks that you do not understand!

Project managers and other project leaders must recognize that it is OK not to understand certain terms and conditions in contracts. In these cases, talk to your office director, Conrad Baumler or myself. I highly recommend that you use Conrad to review contracts that you have not seen before or terms and conditions

you do not understand. Use these opportunities to learn about risk and risk allocation.

2. Don't accept responsibility for things that are beyond your control!

Obvious examples for design professionals include construction site safety and means and methods of construction. We do not control these things – the contractor does. This also includes the alliance subcontractor for a designer-led-design-build project. Therefore, we should not accept risk for these things. Remember — if you don't control it, don't accept the risk!

3. Don't accept responsibility for things someone else messes up!

Client contracts often contain clauses that have us indemnifying the client for the *client's errors*. This is not reasonable. We should only indemnify clients and others for *our negligent* acts, errors and omissions. Remember — if someone else messes it up, they should have the risk!

4. Don't bet the company on any one project!

Any one project is only worth so much risk to the company. How much is that? It depends and, of course, requires judgment. However, accepting a project risk that could bring down the company, is obviously too much. Sometimes we just have to walk away from opportunities because they are not worth it. ▲

BEST PRACTICES

THIS COLUMN IS INTENDED TO SHARE SOME BEST PRACTICES THAT WE HAVE SEEN AROUND THE COMPANY OR HAVE LEARNED FROM OUTSIDE SOURCES. SCOTT BRALEY, AIA AND PROJECT MANAGEMENT CONSULTANT TO THE A/E INDUSTRY, DEFINES BEST PRACTICE AS THOSE ACTIONS THE FIRM TAKES TO GET THE BEST RESULTS IN THE INDUSTRY. SO PARAPHRASING BRALEY, THIS COLUMN IS ABOUT THOSE ACTIONS INDIVIDUALS ARE TAKING TO GET THE BEST RESULTS IN THE FIRM. OUR GOAL IS FOR THESE PRACTICES TO BECOME THE BEST IN THE INDUSTRY. –DEM

Identify Responsible Charge Team Members for each Discipline – Most projects at Shive-Hattery require that a licensed professional architect, landscape architect, engineer or land surveyor certify the documents (plans, specifications, reports, surveys, etc.). Many projects require that licensed professionals representing various disciplines certify applicable portions of the documents. Sometimes core team members (those team members who perform most of the work on a project) are not licensed professionals. In these situations, the project manager must identify and recruit a licensed professional to join the project team who will supervise the work and will certify the final documents. *The licensed professional should be on the project team from beginning through the end.* This practice will provide better direction for the core team members and will result in less rework. Documents can easily be certified when their preparation is complete, because the design professional is already familiar with them. This is not only a *Best Practice*, but is the spirit of the law. *Is this your practice on your projects?*

SUBMIT YOUR BEST PRACTICE TO DALE MOORE FOR FUTURE ISSUES OF PROJECT DELIVERY.

Client Focused Proposals – We talk a lot about preparing proposals focused on the client. Many of our project leaders are doing this in one way or another. Recently, I saw one of the *best practices* of this idea that I may have ever seen. Bill Cary, project manager and transportation leader in the Cedar Rapids office, prepared a proposal for the City of Marion for the planning phase of the 29th Avenue corridor extension for the city. Mike Duffy, civil engineer for the Cedar Rapids community development team, used Publisher to create a 11 x 17 report format that was only three pages long. The document included electronically imported photographs and other "eye catching" graphics. While the document addressed the usual items like project understanding, project approach, elements of the proposal (scope, schedule, fee), team capabilities and previous experience, it did so in a way that gave the client the feel we were talking about their project. Perhaps the photographs, which are always in view, helped to create that feeling. In addition, the proposal addressed the client's hot button issues. Our $25,000 proposal was chosen over Ament's $18,000 proposal. City Engineer Erv Mussman told the City Council that he recommended the more expensive proposal because the mix of people who would work on the team including a landscape architect who would look at the aesthetics and safety issues that blend with the technical side of the project. *For more detail, contact Bill Cary in the Cedar Rapids office.*

fact: We have been publishing project manager performance results for the three primary stakeholder groups for ten months. The amount of data for team member satisfaction varies significantly among the project managers. Of those who have been a designated project manager all ten months, eight have received data six to nine of the ten months, eight have received data three to five of the ten months, and eight have received data two or fewer months in this period. Project Managers: are you collecting enough data?

WE JUDGE OURSELVES BY WHAT WE FEEL CAPABLE OF DOING, WHILE OTHERS JUDGE US BY WHAT WE HAVE ALREADY DONE. – HENRY WADSWORTH LONGFELLOW

A MANAGER...SETS OBJECTIVES...ORGANIZES...MOTIVATES...COMMUNICATES...MEASURES... AND DEVELOPS PEOPLE. EVERY MANAGER DOES THESE THINGS — KNOWINGLY OR NOT. A MANAGER MAY DO THEM WELL, OR MAY DO THEM WRETCHEDLY, BUT ALWAYS DOES THEM. – PETER DRUCKER

TEAM MEMBERS ALWAYS EVALUATE THE PROJECT MANAGER'S PERFORMANCE. THE RESULTS MAY OR MAY NOT BE RECORDED. HOW CAN PROJECT MANAGERS GET BETTER IF THEY DON'T KNOW HOW TEAM MEMBERS RATE THEIR PERFORMANCE? – DALE MOORE

MYTHS OF DESIGN-BUILD

Jerry Novacek of Zweig-White & Associates

THE FOLLOWING IS AN ARTICLE REPRINTED BY PERMISSION OF ZWEIG-WHITE & ASSOCIATES, A LEADING CONSULTANT TO THE DESIGN PROFESSIONAL INDUSTRY. THE ARTICLE APPEARED IN THE FEBRUARY 8, 1999 ISSUE OF *DESIGN-BUILD ADVISOR* PUBLISHED BY ZWEIG-WHITE.

IN GENERAL, I AGREE WITH JERRY NOVACEK'S OBSERVATIONS. MY PERSONAL OPINION OF THE THREE MYTHS CAN BE SUMMARIZED AS FOLLOWS:

- OWNERS DON'T ALWAYS SAVE MONEY USING THE DESIGN-BUILD DELIVERY SYSTEM. HOWEVER, OWNERS SHOULD ACHIEVE A BENEFIT (LIKE SCHEDULE OR COST) IF THEY SELECT DESIGN-BUILD.
- OWNERS DON'T ELIMINATE RISKS BY SELECTING THE DESIGN-BUILD DELIVERY MODEL, NOR SHOULD THEY. RISKS SHOULD ALWAYS BE ALLOCATED TO THE PRINCIPLE PROJECT PLAYERS (OWNER, DESIGN PROFESSIONAL, CONTRACTOR, ETC.) IN PROPORTION TO THEIR POTENTIAL REWARDS. (REFER TO THE ARTICLE ON PAGE ONE OF THIS ISSUE OF *PROJECT DELIVERY*.)
- DESIGN-BUILD IS HERE TO STAY, BUT WILL NEVER REPLACE THE OTHER PRIMARY PROJECT DELIVERY SYSTEMS — DESIGN-AWARD-BUILD AND CONSTRUCTION MANAGEMENT. -DEM

Consumer benefits and risks exist for every product, whether it's a new car, brand of cereal, or type of toothpaste. In fact, most advertisers will tell you that the perception of a product is what sells it. The product may or may not meet your needs but an expectation of what it will do develops in the marketplace. The advertising leads you to believe that it will solve all your problems. It's the "one size fits all" mentality.

The same thing has happened with the design/build delivery method over the last five years. We know one size doesn't fit all in the consumer or professional services business. Yet many people have unrealistic expectations or perceptions of what design/build will do for them. Owners, A/E/Ps, and contractors who have never used design/build do not understand it. Therefore, false expectations and myths have developed in the marketplace. Here are three of the most significant design/build myths and the reasons why they're not true:

Owners always save money.

We've talked about the "drivers" of the design/build market. We've said the most important drivers were schedule, cost, quality, single point of responsibility, operations, and financing. Owners today are most concerned about the number of lawsuits, the increasing cost of the design and construction process, and the time it takes to deliver new capital improvement projects— especially in the public sector.

What we have experienced is that owners do not always save money when they use design/build. This is especially true in the public sector and when the project is schedule driven by the owner. There are new and different risks associated with completing a design/build project for both the design and construction companies. Because of these risks and the new working relationship, a contingency must be provided for these costs — costs that increase what the owner will pay for the improvements. We predict, however, that once design/build teams have worked together and more clients understand design/build, these costs will turn into savings for the owner.

Owners eliminate their risks.

In both the private and public market sectors we see more and more owners using purchasing departments, risk management personnel, and contract terms and conditions to eliminate or reduce their risks. In fact, owners are hiring both A/E/P firms and lawyers (bridging firms) who are telling them they should be able to eliminate theirs risks by using design/build as their project delivery method.

No matter what anybody tells you, design/build does not eliminate the owner's risk. Common sense tells you that every party to a contract (design/build or traditional design-bid-build) will have project risks. The key success factor is only assuming the risks that are yours and that you are capable of managing. The advantage of a design/build contract is that the contractor and A/E/P firm have agreed to work together so the risks associated with their working relationship are not the owner's.

A word of caution is needed at this point. We have the experience of knowing and working with both A/E/P and legal firms who, as the owners' consultants, are taking advantage of the design/build team and deliver process. Instead of defining the owner's risks and assisting in their management, consultants are asking the design/build team to assume these risks. The result? Project costs increases significantly and/or re-negotiation of these risks occurs so late in the selection process that design/build teams are unable to submit a proposal or bid. In fact, many times these negotiations may not be completed until right before the final bid date. At this point all of the short-listed design/build teams have experienced significant costs all because they have been asked to assume the owner's risks. Remember, the proper "professional bridging" A/E/P or law consultant will be working to build trust in the best interest of everyone involved with the project. Early in the proposal process they will conduct a risk assessment and determine the owner's and the design/build team's risks. The design/build team will then have the time and information necessary to evaluate and mitigate the risks and submit a proposal or bid.

Design/build is a fad and it will disappear in a few years.

Design/build has been used in the private sector for many years. When people say design/build is a fad, most are referring to the government or public sector marketplace. These people believe that it will not become a preferred project delivery method. What they don't know is that government agencies such as the Army Corps of Engineers and Department of Defense have used design/build since the early 1970s. More and more local, city, county, and state governments are using design/build. As of 1997 the FAR regulations allow for design/build, and other federal agencies are using or are planning to use it soon.

Five years ago more than 30 states were silent or did not allow design/build as a project delivery method in the public sector. Today the opposite is true: Over 30 states now allow design/build. In several states where legislation has not been approved, they are evaluating design/build by approving a limited number of projects. What is important is the growth of design/build over this same period of time. Market analysis group F.W. Dodge reported that the number of design/build projects increased over 20% and the size of the projects over $5 million increased over 37% for all 12 construction market sectors in 1997. In fact, the total dollar volume was well over $23 billion.

With this increase it is apparent that many clients prefer or are willing to use this delivery method versus the traditional design-bid-build process. Lastly, we are becoming a global economy and design/build is the preferred delivery method of developing countries. Because of this, many more private domestic clients will be forced to use design/build to complete their projects faster so they can compete more effectively overseas.

— Jerry Novacek (jnovacek@zwa.com) ▲

TOOLS AND TIPS

SUBMIT YOUR TOOL TIPS TO DALE MOORE FOR FUTURE ISSUES OF PROJECT DELIVERY.

Getting Magazines Circulated –

Periodicals like *PM Network*, PMI's monthly magazine for project leaders, are full of information and ideas that will help you become a better project manager, team member or project sponsor. Of course, you have to plan for time to read them to receive the benefit. The problem multiplies when circulating one copy of a monthly magazine to several people in the office. The Moline office project managers have found an efficient way to circulate the office copy of *PM Network*. Each month one PM is assigned to receive the magazine first. That person reads the magazine and highlights the more pertinent information in a timely manner. As the magazine is circulated, the highlighting allows the other PMs to review it more quickly.

AutoCAD Training for Managers – Do

the project leaders in your office understand the basics of AutoCAD and how our drawings get produced? The answer is more often no than it is yes. The Iowa City office under the leadership of Don Bruce decided to do something about that situation. Don conducted an in-house training course for project managers and the office management team covering the basics of AutoCAD. The purpose of the course was to provide a basic understanding of how the drawings get produced and to give the project leaders the capability of reviewing drawings on line during production. *This is a good idea that can easily be implemented in all offices.*

Are you using MSP and Critical Tools?

– If you are a project manager and are not using Microsoft Project and Critical Tools on some of your projects, you should be! These are great planning, communications and tracking tools. And — with a little experimentation and practice, they are easy to use. Yes, I am serious! You should be able to input a 30 to 45 line item schedule and "clean it up" for printing in about one hour. This includes activity, duration, resource names and precedence. *If you need help, contact Dale Moore.* I would be happy to meet with you and help you get started or to upgrade your knowledge. I am not an expert, but my knowledge and abilities with these two software products is rapidly increasing. Why? Because I use it!

COMING SOON!

TWO EDUCATION OPPORTUNITIES FOR PROJECT LEADERS

Two education opportunities will be available in late summer and fall for project leaders (project managers, office directors, team leaders, office managers and others selected by the office director) throughout the Company. These courses are:

Designer-Led Project Delivery

This course is intended to teach the basic philosophy and processes of Shive-Hattery Construction and to equip project managers with a basic understanding of our project management role in leading both the design and construction process.

Current schedule for the approximate 3.5-hour course is:

Iowa City Office ....July 21		Des Moines Office ....August 11
Moline Office ....July 26		Bloomington and Chicago Offices........August 12
Cedar Rapids Office ....August 4		(@ Bloomington)

PMs who cannot attend the session in their office, can make arrangements to attend at another offic

Course topics include:
- Company philosophy of design-build project delivery.
- Understanding project delivery systems and roles.
- Shive-Hattery Construction designer-led design-build process.
- How does general contracting work?
- How do we lead both the design and the construction?
- Managing the design and construction contract.

Instructors are Rick Berndt, Conrad Baumler and Dale Moore

The Business of Project Management

This course is intended to equip project managers and other project leaders with the business knowledge required in leading projects. The course will be given in two 2.5-day sessions.

Session 1:   August 25 (1/2 day), 26 & 27 City Plaza Hotel, Iowa City
Session 2:   October 18 (1/2 day), 19 & 20 City Plaza Hotel, Iowa City

Course Outline Includes:

Module 1 Understanding Firm Finances
- Firm finances
- Role of the project manager
- Benchmarking

Module 2 The Project Manager's Business Responsibility
- Decision to go or not to go
- Managing risk
- Managing cash flow (billings and collections)
- Obtaining the written contract
- Managing quality

Module 3 The Project Team
- Review reading assignments
- The role, qualities and responsibilities of team members
- Recruiting your project team

Module 4 Getting the Next Job
- What is marketing?
- Evolving A/E marketing model
- The role of project delivery in marketing
- The three organizational models
- Why do we lose clients?
- The role of the PM in marketing

Instructors include Conrad Baumler, Anne Cameron, Jim Cutler, Tom Hayden, Dale Moore, Steve Noack and Guy Patten.

PROJECT DELIVERY

VOLUME I   ISSUE 5   AUGUST 1999

▲ SHIVE·HATTERY   INFORMATION ON PROJECT MANAGEMENT, DESIGNER-LED
DESIGN-BUILD AND OTHER PROJECT DELIVERY ISSUES

HOW DO YOU BUILD PROJECT MANAGEMENT COMPETENCE THROUGHOUT AN ORGANIZATION?

THE KEY IS FOCUSING ON THREE AREAS OF PROJECT MANAGEMENT COMPETENCE!

Dale Moore

INSIDE:

BEST PRACTICES

SPECS & DETAILS

LESSONS FROM A SUCCESSFUL PROJECT

TOOLS AND TIPS

BUSINESS OF PM COURSE

FOR MORE INFORMATION OR SUGGESTIONS CONTACT:

DALE MOORE
CORPORATE OFFICE
OPX 170
319.362.0313
INTERNAL E-MAIL

Thomas Block, vice president of PM Solutions, and J. Davidson Fame, author and professor, suggest that for organizations to complete projects effectively, they must achieve competence in project management in three areas of the organization — the individual project manager, the team and the organization itself. (See the diagram below.) They also suggest that strengthening competence in one area will be less effective without achieving competence in the other areas as well. So what does it mean for an organization, like Shive-Hattery, to be competent in each of the three areas? And what are we doing to achieve competence in the three areas at Shive-Hattery?

THREE AREAS OF PROJECT MANAGEMENT COMPETENCE

Individual Project Manager Competence

Block and Fame say organizations need to focus on building individual competence in three areas – knowledge-based competence, socially rooted competence and business judgement competence. In a nutshell, these areas include:

- Knowledge-based competence includes knowledge in nine project management body of knowledge (PMBOK) areas and associated tools and processes.

- Socially rooted competence involves skills such as leadership, communication and dealing with people.
- Business competence involves understanding and following practices that are consistent with the interest of the business of our organization. Practices such as deciding what projects to accept, getting contracts, managing quality, managing risks, billing and collections.

What are we doing at Shive-Hattery?
Here are some of the initiatives:
- Project management leadership development class.
- Education and training for project leaders. In 1998, we focused on PMBOK basic skills, MS Project and project planning. In 1999, we are focusing on tracking and controlling, behavior styles training and the business of project management (see the back cover for details of this course).
- Project management processes using the PMBOK Guide and the Shive-Hattery process manual (which is in need of improvement).
- Measurement of performance by the three stakeholder groups and coaching for improved performance.

What do we at Shive-Hattery need to do better and faster?
We need to identify and develop a cadre of good project managers (10-12) across the company who are on a track to become professional project managers. A professional project manager manages projects most of the time and is a competent professional in the field.

continued on back

BEST PRACTICES

THIS COLUMN IS INTENDED TO SHARE SOME BEST PRACTICES THAT WE HAVE SEEN AROUND THE COMPANY OR HAVE LEARNED FROM OUTSIDE SOURCES. SCOTT BRALEY, AIA AND PROJECT MANAGEMENT CONSULTANT TO THE A/E INDUSTRY, DEFINES BEST PRACTICE AS THOSE ACTIONS THE FIRM TAKES TO GET THE BEST RESULTS IN THE INDUSTRY. SO PARAPHRASING BRALEY, THIS COLUMN IS ABOUT THOSE ACTIONS INDIVIDUALS ARE TAKING TO GET THE BEST RESULTS IN THE FIRM. OUR GOAL IS FOR THESE PRACTICES TO BECOME THE BEST IN THE INDUSTRY. –DEM

SUBMIT YOUR BEST PRACTICE TO DALE MOORE FOR FUTURE ISSUES OF PROJECT DELIVERY.

Quick Letter Contracts – The Des Moines office has developed a short form contract for project leaders to carry in their briefcases. They call the form a quick letter contract, because they fill out the document and get the clients signature in the field. One primary purpose of the document is getting contracts for additional services. Change order contracts are often overlooked. *Contact Anne Cameron, Des Moines office manager, for more details and a sample of the quick letter contract.*

Negotiate Change Orders Before Billing the Client – Peg Rabe, corporate office, spends a significant amount of time contacting clients when payment for invoiced services is slow. One of the more common causes she finds for delayed payment is when we have invoiced for additional services, but have not obtained a change order for the additional services. These situations create additional work for several people and irritate the client. Create enough opportunities for irritations and soon you will have a dissatisfied client. It is an absolute necessity for project managers to obtain clear approval and a meeting of the minds for additional costs before invoicing for services. Ideally, the project manager should have a signed change order from the client before the invoice is sent. If not, include two copies of the change order with a Shive-Hattery signature in the same envelope as the invoice. Also send a short letter documenting the client's approval of the additional services and cost. Request that the client sign the change order for his and our records and send one copy back to us. *Professional project managers will consistently make this a best practice.*

Don't Leave Planning Sessions or Project Meetings Without Getting Commitments – Have you ever held a planning session or other type of project meeting and left without getting commitments? People often postpone making commitments for many reasons — to retain freedom, to consult others, to get more data, etc. You have heard all of these reasons and more. Fred Erman, PMP with 25 years experience leading projects for AT&T, IT&T and consulting firms says, "Don't let people leave meetings without making commitments." Here is what Mr. Erman suggests you do to *always get commitments*:

For example, a person may say, "I have to review this further before giving a date." You reply, "Does two days seem reasonable for your review?" If agreed, mark that as an expected date. If not, determine what is reasonable and mark that date. Now you have a DFD (date for a date). If getting a DFD is difficult, don't give up. If you are told, "I don't know how long it will take for review," ask, "Can you look this over and tell me tomorrow how much review time you will need?" After agreement, you will have a DFDFD (a date for a date for a date). Then you will know when to expect the DFD. Now you are in control!

Erman also suggests that you teach people the terminology so you can simply ask, What's the DFD?" Or ask, "What's the DFDFD?" When these terms are used, you will get commitments, not excuses or stalls!

Getting Everyone Involved in Project Management – The Cedar Rapids office management team (OMT) and project management group (PM) spent a couple of their June meetings determining how to involve all team members in project management. They decided the process would start with sharing more information and teaching. Here are some of the specific action items they are implementing:

- Place posters around the office containing the nine PMI PM knowledge areas.
- Distribute copies of *Project Delivery* to the entire office.
- Invite team members to the biweekly PM meetings.
- Distribute copies of the PM meeting notes to all team members.
- Review the basics of the PMI PM Knowledge areas with team members through "lunch and learn" sessions.
- Recognize and reward the use of PM tools.
- Review the performance results with all team members.

LESSONS FROM A SUCCESSFUL PROJECT

Bruce Harding

BRUCE HARDING, PROJECT MANAGER IN THE MOLINE OFFICE, CONDUCTED A POST-PROJECT ANALYSIS FOR A LARGE PROJECT COMPLETED FOR VON MAUR, INC. THIS PAST SPRING. THE PROJECT INCLUDED A REMODEL OF THE VON MAUR CORPORATE HEAD-QUARTERS FACILITY AND A MAJOR ADDITION TO THE MAIN DISTRIBUTION CENTER. BRUCE INCLUDED 13 OTHER TEAM MEMBERS IN THE ANALYSIS. THE PROJECT WAS VERY SUCCESSFUL AS MEASURED BY ALL THREE STAKEHOLDER GROUPS. CONGRATULATIONS TO BRUCE AND THE REST OF THE TEAM. — DEM

The Von Maur project team conducted a post-project analysis at the completion of the construction document and bidding phases. Eight of the nine areas of the *Project Management Body of Knowledge (PMBOK)* were used as a topic outline for our analysis. The following are a few highlights of the lessons we learned from five of the PMBOK areas:

Integration The precedence diagram is a good scheduling tool particularly when the project team is from several offices. Task relationships need to be shown between disciplines in order to identify the true critical paths. If problems are identified during meetings, resolve the problem. If this is not possible, the PM must follow-up relentlessly until the problem is resolved.

Scope The project master plan drawings (the base plan for the project) must be updated on a regular periodic basis. A team member should be assigned to this responsibility.

Time Include client representatives in the initial scheduling meeting. It is beneficial to conduct weekly meetings with the client prior to conducting weekly internal meetings.

Cost Discipline leaders must be responsible for developing cost estimates for their discipline. The PM is responsible for integrating the discipline cost estimates into a project cost estimate.

Quality A team member needs to be assigned to review the entire set of project documents. Specification writers need to complete their sections two weeks before completion of the drawings so the support team members will have adequate time to complete the processing of the specifications. One person should complete divisions 0 and 1.▲

RESEARCH DATA: A study performed in 1997 by Penn State University forecasts that the number of projects delivered using the design-build project delivery system will continue to increase. In 1985, only five percent of projects were delivered using design-build. Today, it is 35 percent. The Penn State study forecasts this will increase to 50 percent by 2010. Most of the increase in design-build delivery will be at the erosion of design-bid-build delivery.

The rise in design-build delivery is just one reason why Shive-Hattery *project leaders* must educate and help owners (clients) select the best delivery system for their project.

"YOU CAN'T STOP THE WAVES, BUT YOU CAN LEARN HOW TO SURF." - ZEN SAYING

"BY THE TIME THE RULES OF THE GAME ARE CLEAR,
THE WINDOWS OF OPPORTUNITY WILL BE CLOSED." - UNKNOWN SOURCE

If Shive-Hattery is to be positioned to lead design and construction projects, project leaders must adapt to new ways of doing business and exhibit these characteristics:

- Think like an owner, like a contractor and like a design professional
- Be entrepreneurial, a creative risk taker
- Have a passion for leading projects.

Another trend in project delivery in the A/E industry is *program management*. Program management is the management of a portfolio of interrelated projects for the same owner (client). Shive-Hattery is the program manager for large building programs for Mercy Medical Center in Cedar Rapids and for the Cedar Rapids Community Schools.

Jerry Allen, CEO of Carter & Burgess, a 1650 person fast growing E/A/P firm, says, "We use to market for projects, but today we are marketing for managed programs." (Incidentally, Carter & Burgess has a group of about 120 project managers and project management-related people who do nothing but manage client projects and programs.)

Reader Feedback: At least two readers, suggested that I was rather bold in the July issue of *Project Delivery* to print one of my own quotes along side quotes from Henry Wadsworth Longfellow and Peter Drucker. I appreciate hearing your comments. Please, send me your feedback and input on *Project Delivery*!

COMPETENCE

continued from front cover

Team Competence

Team competence can be defined as those traits that enable teams to operate quickly and cost effectively and to develop superior solutions to problems. The degree to which the team is competent has a major bearing on whether a project is successful or not.

What are we doing in Shive-Hattery?
We clearly need to do more, but the following are some of our focus areas:

- Involving team members in the up front project planning process.
- Providing behavior styles training for all team members.
- Focusing on core project teams. Core team members are those who will perform the majority of the project work and focus on one or two projects with a minimum of multi-tasking.

Organizational Competence

Organizational competence is a reflection of an organization's ability to create an environment that supports project managers and team members to do the best job possible. For more on this subject, I invite you to read the book *Creating an Environment for Successful Projects* by Robert Graham and Randall Englund.

What are we doing at Shive-Hattery?
The list of things we are doing is quite impressive. Here are some of the areas of emphasis that support an environment for successful projects:

- Leadership training for team leaders with Dr. Judd West
- Project management leadership development class
- Other leadership groups
- Career development program
- Discipline groups focused on our work processes
- Standard specifications and reference details
- Project management processes
- Continued advancement of technology (Examples include the Intranet, Internet, software, and hardware.)

The annual business planning time is coming soon. I invite you to share your ideas on what you think is important in building competence in project management and project delivery! - DEM ▲

TOOLS AND TIPS

SUBMIT YOUR TOOL TIPS TO DALE MOORE FOR FUTURE ISSUES OF PROJECT DELIVE

Assessing the Adequacy and Completeness of Your WBS – The following i list of questions, suggested by William Duncan of Project Management Partners, you can use assess the adequacy and completeness of your next WBS:

- Do the items at the lower level completely define the item at the upper level?
- Does the lowest level provide adequate detail to estimate time, cost and duration?
- Can you assign a single source responsibility to each item at the lowest level?
- Are management activities included?
- Are integration activities included?

Consider Using CSI Divisions of Work to Define Your WBS – Walt Disney Imagineering (WDI) uses CSI construction divisions to define their WBS for facility design a construction projects. For more details, refer to an article appearing on pages 31 to 36 of July 1999 issue of *PM Network*.

Are You Using Earned Value Analysis? – If you are a project manager and are n using an earned value analysis (or some other process) to monitor and control your mediu and large size projects, you should be! Earned value offers an excellent methology to monit a project's progress in terms of time, cost and scope in an integrated fashion. This method capable of providing a project manager early warning signs of project overruns — as early 15 to 20 percent into the project. If you need help getting started, contact Dale Moore for h *Project managers who are not using an acceptable monitoring and controlling tool an process are not doing project management!*

COMING SOON!
BUSINESS OF PROJECT MANAGEMENT COURSE

This course is intended to equip project managers and other project leaders with the busines knowledge required to lead projects. The course will be given twice. Each session is 2.5 days and will be held at the City Plaza Hotel in Iowa City.

Session 1: August 25 (1/2 day), 26, & 27
Session 2: October 18 (1/2 day), 19, & 20

Course Outline Includes:

Module 1 Understanding Firm Finances
- Firm finances
- Role of the project manager
- Benchmarking

Module 2 The Project Manager's Business Responsibility
- Decision to go or not to go
- Managing risk
- Managing cash flow (billings and collections)
- Obtaining the written contract
- Managing quality

Module 3 The Project Team
- Review reading assignments
- The role, qualities, and responsibilities of team members
- Recruiting your project team

Module 4 Getting the Next Job
- What is marketing?
- Evolving A/E marketing model
- Why do we lose clients?
- The three organizational models
- The role of project delivery in marketin
- The role of the PM in marketing

Instructors include Conrad Baumler, Anne Cameron, Jim Cutler, Tom Hayden, Dale Moor Steve Noack and Guy Patten.

SHIVE·HATTERY

VOLUME I   ISSUE 6

SEPTEMBER 1999

SHIVE·HATTERY

INFORMATION ON PROJECT MANAGEMENT, DESIGNER-LED
DESIGN-BUILD AND OTHER PROJECT DELIVERY ISSUES

MAINTAING THE BIG PICTURE PERSPECTIVE

FIVE BASIC PRINCIPLES FOR SUCCESSFUL PROJECT MANAGERS

Dale Moore

**FOR MORE INFORMATION
OR SUGGESTIONS
CONTACT:**

**DALE MOORE
CORPORATE OFFICE
OPX 170
319.362.0313
INTERNAL E-MAIL**

Those of you who manage projects know that it is easy to get caught up in the helter-skelter of putting out fires and focusing on the minutiae of detail on a project. When this happens, the project manager loses sight of the big picture perspective of the project. Project management is about leading others to work toward a successful project. It becomes exceedingly difficult to effectively lead others when you are caught up in all of the detail.

So how does one stay focused on the big picture and avoid the temptation to get involved in all of the detail? In his book, *Managing Projects in Organizations,* J. Davidson Fame suggests there are five basic principles for project managers to follow to keep focused on the big picture. Here are his principles coupled with some of my thoughts:

1. **Be conscious of what you are doing; don't be an accidental project manager** – Projects are hard to manage even when you know what you are doing. They are nearly impossible to manage by accident when you are only focused on one aspect of the project like design. This is why we need a core group of professional project managers who are focused on the job of managing our large and medium-sized projects. All professional project managers should

understand and practice project management principles. Then they will be less likely to get sucked into the details of the design of the project.

2. **Invest heavily in the front-end spadework; get it right the first time** – It takes time to determine the *real* needs of the customer. Without this effort, it is increasingly likely that the final deliverable will not be what the customer is expecting. Projects must also be carefully planned to ensure that work is not accomplished out of sequence. Working out of sequence can substantially increase the chances of inefficiencies, waste and rework. But don't underestimate the extent of the front-end spadework. Professional project managers know the value of replanning the project after about 15 percent of the work is complete. At this point, you really begin to understand the requirements of the project. Refinement in plans at this point can be invaluable.

3. **Anticipate the problems that will inevitably arise** – Schedule and budget variances will always occur—it is impossible to precisely predict the future. Customer needs will change. Even project goals and objectives may change. Professional project mangers understand these potential problems before they arise and know how to cope with these changes.

(continued on page two)

BEST PRACTICES

THIS COLUMN IS INTENDED TO SHARE SOME BEST PRACTICES THAT WE HAVE SEEN AROU[ND]
THE COMPANY OR HAVE LEARNED FROM OUTSIDE SOURCES. SCOTT BRALEY, AIA AND PROJE[CT]
MANAGEMENT CONSULTANT TO THE A/E INDUSTRY, DEFINES BEST PRACTICES AS THOSE [AC]
TIONS THE FIRM TAKES TO GET THE BEST RESULTS IN THE INDUSTRY. SO PARAPHRASING BRAL[EY]
THIS COLUMN IS ABOUT THOSE ACTIONS INDIVIDUALS ARE TAKING TO GET THE BEST RESULTS [FOR]
THE FIRM. OUR GOAL IS FOR THESE PRACTICES TO BECOME THE BEST IN THE INDUSTRY. —D[EM]

Are You Sharing Best Practices Across the Company? – In the book, *The Boundaryless Organi[za]tion,* the authors suggest that one trait of service companies who have successfully broken down horizo[ntal] boundaries is that "each team in the firm shares best practices with other teams, so that all clients ben[efit] from the knowledge and ideas gleaned from particular (experiences)." How well are you doin[g] sharing your best practices with others in the Company? I would be delighted to hear from you and [be] able to share your best practices in the next issue of *Project Delivery*!

Mechanical Discipline Group Develops Several Productivity Tools – The Mechani[cal] Discipline Group, under the leadership of Chris Nelson, has developed several new tools [that] will significantly enhance the productivity of our mechanical designs. These tools include:

SUBMIT YOUR
BEST PRACTICE TO
DALE MOORE FOR
FUTURE ISSUES OF
PROJECT DELIVERY.

- Typical schematic design and design development phase narratives (this document can be used like a master specification section).
- 31 reference schedules.
- A standard construction review sheet (things to look for during construction observation visits).
- A master list of typical construction punch list items (things to look for in the field).

The effort by this group should be the model for other discipline groups. Contact Chris Nelson in the [Des] Moines office for more details.

Project Kickoff – The Meeting You Never Want to Miss – Kathleen Demery, PMP, manager [of] Software Engineering for ALLTEL Information Services says, "A successful project kickoff meeting will r[ally] the team, get everyone focused, gain team member commitment, clarify roles and responsibilities, and [set] the tone for the entire project." Are you missing this opportunity on your projects?

BIG PICTURE
continued from front cover

4. **Go beneath surface illusions; dig deeply to find the real situation** – Customers usually do not have a clear concept of th[eir] needs when the project begins even if they think they do. Project managers who blindly accept customer needs statements m[ay] produce a deliverable the customer does not really want. While this may seem to be a customer problem, they may not see it that w[ay.] Customers feel that we are design professionals and should know what questions to ask. We should lead the customer in the corr[ect] direction. Professional project managers do not accept initial customer requirements at face value. Professional project managers [will] ask the probing questions and offer professional advice based on experience that will help the customer arrive at his real needs.

5. **Be as flexible as possible; don't get sucked into unnecessary rigidity and formality** – The natural state of a projec[t is] chaos. Good project managers strive to create order out of the chaos. The drive to create order may, however, lead to the ris[k of] sacrificing reasonable flexibility. We may convince ourselves that the more structure we impose on the project the less chaos we [will] face. In our attempt to impose structure to achieve order, we may instead achieve stifling bureaucracy. Things will always change [on] projects; therefore, a reasonable amount of flexibility is needed. Professional project managers will learn to strike a balance betw[een] the need for order and the contrary need for flexibility. –DEM

WHY HAVE A WRITTEN CONTRACT?

ONLY THREE OUT OF FOUR PROJECTS AT SHIVE-HATTERY HAVE A WRITTEN CONTRACT! OUR GOAL IS TO HAVE ALL PROJECTS UNDER CONTRACT. THIS IS ONE OF OUR PROJECT MANAGEMENT PERFORMANCE MEASURES. THERE ARE MANY REASONS FOR HAVING CONTRACTS. THE FOLLOWING, REPRINTED WITH THE PERMISSION OF DPIC (OUR PROFESSIONAL LIABILITY INSURANCE CARRIER), IS DPIC'S TOP FOUR REASONS FOR HAVING CONTRACTS FOR OUR PROFESSIONAL SERVICES. WE NEED TO HAVE MORE CONTRACTS FOR OUR PROJECTS AT SHIVE-HATTERY! —DEM

This article is adapted from DPIC's Contract Guide: A Risk Management Handbook for Architectural, Engineering and Environmental Profesesionals, with permisssion from DPIC Companies, Inc.

The construction process involves a complex series of relationships. Owners, contractors, subcontractors, material suppliers, fabricators, environmental consultants, architects, engineers, subconsultants, construction managers, program managers– all may be involved in today's construction project. With so many parties, each under intense pressure to provide more service for less money, it is essential that everyone understands his or her role and responsibilities. That is the primary function of a contract– to memorialize these understandings.

Here are the primary benefits of written contracts:

1. *Mutual understanding.* The process of developing the scope of services, compensation, schedule and terms by which you will operate requires you and your client to communicate your own views on each of these issues. As a result, both of you will derive a better understanding of the other's needs and concerns. And better understanding promotes better relationships. After all, if you and your client can't agree on basic terms of a contract, how could you hope to work together under the pressures encountered during a project?

2. *Establishing your own rules.* When a contract is silent on certain issues, the law may impose its own default condition to address those issues. For example, when a contract does not specify how a dispute will be resolved, the default is generally to the civil court system, and either party can institute litigation. But you and your client can agree by contract to use some other dispute resolution mechanism, such as mediation or arbitration, instead of the courts. Similarly, parties to a contract can agree that neither will sue the other for *consequential damages* or that the period during which either can initiate a claim is shorter than may otherwise be allowed by the applicable statutes of repose or limitation. Bear in mind that the ability to establish your own rules does not permit you to specify measures that are against public policy or are illegal. Nevertheless, setting your own rules can eliminate or at least lessen problems that might otherwise arise.

3. *Sizing up your client.* It is important to understand your client's attitudes and motivations. The process of contract formation and negotiation allows you to assess the people with whom you are dealing and decide whether you want to work with them. Beware of clients who have little compunction about sacrificing quality or unfairly shifting their own liabilities to you. Does the client have a realistic budget and schedule? What is the client's experience with this type of project? Is the client sophisticated or will you have to spend a lot of time educating and hand-holding? Why did the client select you? How will the contractors be chosen? Does the client have a reputation for slow payment (or nonpayment) of fees? Does the client have a history of claims and litigation? What does your "gut" tell you about the client? Exercise great care in selecting your clients; it is one of the best loss prevention tools at your disposal.

4. *Identifying and allocating risk.* The process of contract formation should always include a candid discussion of the project risks. It's also easier to evaluate a client's attitudes and motivations when the subject of risk is brought up at the beginning of the relationship. This helps assure that risk reduction and risk handling mechanisms are incorporated into the workscope as well as the business terms and conditions of the contract. For instance, who should bear the risk of redesign if construction bids exceed the budget? Who should bear the risk of changes to your design by others and without your knowledge? Who bears the risk if your documents are reused to build another iteration of the structure you designed? Does your prospective client intend to use its economic power to force you to accept an unreasonable share of the project risk? Or is the client willing to consider the risks and rewards from your perspective as well, and to seek a fair position in which you can both succeed?

TOOLS AND TIPS

SUBMIT YOUR TOOL TIPS TO DALE MOORE FOR FUTURE ISSUES OF *PROJECT DELIVERY*.

Are Reference Details used on your projects? – The use of reference details can improve efficiencies and, thus, lower costs on any project. Project managers should insist that discipline leaders use them to the fullest extent possible. Reference details can be identified on finished drawings by a reference code located on the right hand side of the detail's title.

Are you identifying risks on your projects? – If you are a project manager and are not using your team to identify potential risks on your projects, you should be! Use the experience of your team to subjectively or quantitatively identify the two or three project risks that will most probably cause 80 percent of the problems on your next project. Then again use your team to identify how to mitigate these risks and build the risk mitigation techniques into your project plan.

Internet Plan Service – US Projects.Com of Omaha, Nebraska provides a new service to architects and engineers by placing bid documents on the Internet for use by contractors and suppliers during bidding processes. They recently presented their approach to our Des Moines office project leaders. For more information on this service, contact Patty Martin at 888-393-4126 or at pattymartin@usprojects.com.

FACT: As of December 31, 1998, membership in the Project Management Institute (PMI) was 43,101. This was up from 31,333 in 1997. *Interest in professional project management is clearly growing.*

Recognition of Design-Build Project Delivery is growing – PMI and the Design-Build Institute of America (DBIA) have executed an agreement of understanding with the purpose of establishing a basis of cooperative efforts between the organizations in areas of common interest and concern.

Project Mangers of the future will need to know their company's business – Harold Kerzner, recognized as the father of project management and author of several recognized books including, *In Search for Excellence in Project Management* says, "We use to believe that if you knew project management, you could go from one industry to the next because the skills of project management are transferable." Kerzner now says, "In the next century, because knowledge of business is so critical, I expect most project management slots to be filled by internal promotions and lateral transfers rather than by hiring people from the outside who might not understand your company culture or even the business you are in."

The Abilene Paradox – In a now famous story, Jerry Harvey tells of a family in Texas who drives 90 miles to Abilene to have a mediocre meal at the cafeteria. They then find they are bored in Abilene, so they immediately drive back home. As they walk back to the house, one of them says, "That was a waste of time!" Another says, "I thought you wanted to go." "No, I only went because the rest of you did." They then survey each other and find that no one really wanted to go. They were fooled by the false consensus effect – silence means consent. This appears to be a failure to manage agreement, but is really a failure to manage disagreement. Project leaders must not fall prey to the Abilene Paradox.

VOLUME I   ISSUE 7   OCTOBER 1999

Shive-Hattery   INFORMATION ON PROJECT MANAGEMENT, DESIGNER-LED DESIGN-BUILD AND OTHER PROJECT DELIVERY ISSUES

ARE YOU A LEADER OR A MANAGER?

By Jim Lewis

THE FOLLOWING ARTICLE APPEARED IN THE SEPTEMBER 1999 ISSUE OF *SUCCESSFUL PROJECT MANAGEMENT* AND IS REPRINTED HERE WITH PERMISSION FROM *SUCCESSFUL PROJECT MANAGEMENT*, VOL. 1, NO. 6, SEPTEMBER 1999, PUBLISHED BY MANAGEMENT CONCEPTS, INC. IN THE ARTICLE, JIM LEWIS TALKS ABOUT THE IMPORTANCE OF LEADERSHIP—IN BEING A PROJECT LEADER—AS WELL AS BEING A MANAGER. AS LEWIS POINTS OUT, SHIVE-HATTERY NEEDS ITS "PROJECT MANAGERS" TO BE BOTH LEADERS AND MANAGERS. HOW ARE YOU DOING? —DEM

INSIDE:

FOR MORE INFORMATION OR SUGGESTIONS CONTACT:

**DALE MOORE
CORPORATE OFFICE
OPX 170
319.362.0313
INTERNAL E-MAIL**

After teaching project management for more than 15 years, I realized recently that most programs like mine are fundamentally flawed. They concentrate on the tools of project management—work breakdown structures, critical path scheduling, earned value analysis, and risk management—but they omit any mention of leadership.

Vance Packard, in *The Pyramid Climbers*, defines leadership as "the art of getting others to want to do something you are convinced should be done." The operative word here is "want." You can get others to do something by coercing them. You can pay them so well they will do even onerous tasks. You can sometimes even shame them into doing things they wouldn't ordinarily want to do. But to get them to want to do something, you have to understand human motivation.

The word "manage" comes originally from French, and meant to handle horses. It now has the connotation of doing the administrative aspects of a job. However, we often use the words "manager" and "leader" synonymously, even though there is a distinc-

tion. We know that not all managers are leaders, and some leaders are not very good managers. A project manager must have both sets of skills.

The simplest way to understand what is required to get others to want to do something is to keep in mind the WIIFM principle: "what's in it for me?" If there is no payoff for the individual in the project activity, then you will have compliance but not motivation. The key to motivation is that we are motivated to engage in certain patterns of activity. For some, it is troubleshooting. Point a troubleshooter toward something that is broken, and she can't wait to fix it. For others it is innovation. These people love to work on improving things. It can be physical things or even systems.

If your organization is like most, people are assigned projects with no regard for WIIFM. They happen to be the closest approximation to the proper skill mix currently available, so they are assigned. When there is really nothing in it for them, we find low levels of commitment and motivation, and wonder what to do about it. The answer, of course, is that if you have a

(continued on page four)

BEST PRACTICES

THIS COLUMN IS INTENDED TO SHARE SOME BEST PRACTICES THAT WE HAVE SE
AROUND THE COMPANY OR HAVE LEARNED FROM OUTSIDE SOURCES. SCOTT BRAL
AIA AND PROJECT MANAGEMENT CONSULTANT TO THE A/E INDUSTRY, DEFINES BE
PRACTICES AS THOSE ACTIONS THE FIRM TAKES TO GET THE BEST RESULTS IN T
INDUSTRY. SO PARAPHRASING BRALEY, THIS COLUMN IS ABOUT THOSE ACTIONS IN
VIDUALS ARE TAKING TO GET THE BEST RESULTS IN THE FIRM. OUR GOAL IS FOR THE
PRACTICES TO BECOME THE BEST IN THE INDUSTRY. —DEM

Project Sponsor Meetings – The Des Moines office has recognized that project sponsors h
significant contact with clients and play a major role in client satisfaction. To help in coordination a
setting priorities for the projects in the office, Des Moines holds a weekly meeting for project sponse
Mike Kammerer reports this is working well. Contact Mike for more details.

Don't Leave Specifications to the Last Minute – Bruce Harding, architect and pro
manager in the Moline office, says that project plans should call for specification writers
complete technical specification sections at least two weeks before the completion of
project. This will allow time for support team members to complete the processing of
specifications and for the overall coordination of the specification set. Bruce also reco
mends that one team member be assigned to complete divisions 0 and 1.

Capitalize on the Strengths of People – Corey Hansen, consultant to the A/E industry, remind
that people do their best job when they are doing what they enjoy and know! It is, therefore, impera
that project managers understand the strengths and desires of team members in making assignme
Hansen says this is most critical with the more experienced senior staff members. Senior team memb
should be assigned tasks that only they can perform, instead of spending their valuable time perform
tasks that could be delegated to other, less experienced, team members.

SUBMIT YOUR BEST PRACTICE TO DALE MOORE FOR FUTURE ISSUES OF *PROJECT DELIVERY.*

TOOLS AND TIPS

SUBMIT YOUR TOOL TIPS TO DALE MOORE FOR FUTURE ISSUES OF *PROJECT DELIVERY.*

Are You Conducting Team Planning Sessions? – Using the entire project team, or at least the core team members, to prepa
project plans still remains one of the most powerful tools for project managers. Team planning has many benefits. Team members w
buy into the plan of attack, the plans are more creative and innovative, planning sessions are excellent team building times and th
planning reduces overall project costs. If you are not using your team to plan projects, you should be!

Include Client Representatives in Team Planning Sessions! – For even more bang for your project planning effort, includ
client representatives in project planning sessions. You'll find out the client's *real* expectations, you'll demonstrate that Shive-Hatte
manages projects professionally and you'll build a stronger relationship with the client.

Look for Ways to Motivate Team Members! – James Lucas in *The Passionate Organization* suggests that project managers ca
help motivate team members by asking a few simple questions such as:
·What turns you on and excites you about your work?
·Why are those things exciting to you?
·What would you like to do more of?
·How can we work together to help develop your skills in these areas?

Know the Behavior and Learning Styles of Your Team Members! – Gloria Frost is nearing the completion of behavior an
learning styles training throughout the Company. This information can be helpful to project managers in leading teams. Contact Glor
to find out the behavior and learning styles of your team members. Or, better yet, ask Gloria how she can help lead your team through
team building exercise where members learn to work effectively with each other's behavior and learning styles. This is a great tool! Use a

WHAT DO CLIENTS AND TEAM MEMBERS EXPECT FROM PROJECT MANAGERS?

By Dale Moore

PROJECT MANAGERS OFTEN ASK, "WHAT DO I NEED TO DO TO PLEASE CLIENTS?" AND, "WHAT DO I NEED TO DO TO PLEASE PROJECT TEAM MEMBERS?" THE ANSWERS AREN'T EASY. IN FACT, THE SATISFACTION OF CLIENTS AND TEAM MEMBERS IS A COMPLEX ISSUE. HOWEVER, I SUGGEST THE FIRST PLACE TO LOOK FOR THE ANSWER IS IN THE CLIENT AND TEAM MEMBER SURVEYS. REVIEW THE SURVEY QUESTIONS LISTED BELOW AND DETERMINE HOW YOU CAN IMPROVE IN EACH OF THE AREAS INCLUDED IN THESE SURVEYS. FOCUSING ON THESE AREAS SHOULD RESULT IN SUBSTANTIAL IMPROVEMENT IN CLIENT AND TEAM MEMBER SATISFACTION. —DEM

Client Service Quality Questionnaire

*Company results through 8/31/99

(1=service did not meet the expectations 3=service was average 5=service exceeded expectations)

1. My expectations were met. **(4.2)**

2. I received value for the fees charged. **(4.1)**

3. Shive-Hattery met my schedule. **(4.2)**

4. Shive-Hattery worked within my budget. **(4.1)**

5. Shive-Hattery was responsive to my needs. **(4.4)**

6. I enjoyed working with Shive-Hattery's staff. **(4.6)**

7. Shive-Hattery addressed project conflict promptly and effectively. **(4.2)**

8. Change orders were not a problem. **(4.2)**

9. How would you rank Shive-Hattery compared to other design firms? **(4.1)**

Team Member Evaluation

*Company results through 8/31/99

(1=strongly disagree 2=disagree 3=generally agree 4=agree 5=strongly agree)

1. Clearly defined and communicated team member roles, responsibilities and accountabilities at the beginning of the project. **(3.9)**

2. Maintained a good relationship with the team members during the project. **(4.2)**

3. Was a good listener who actively sought team member ideas and solutions for how to deliver this project. **(4.1)**

4. Proactively developed and maintained backup strategies (contingency plans) in anticipation of potential project problems. **(3.7)**

5. Used a workable set of project planning, project re-planning and control tools. **(3.7)**

6. Continuously stressed to project team members the importance of meeting budget, schedule commitments and customer (internal and external) expectations. **(4.0)**

7. Was readily accessible to team members. **(4.0)**

8. Kept the project team informed in a timely manner. **(3.9)**

9. Was willing to help people realize their full potential; tried to bring out the best in people. **(4.0)**

10. Was timely and effective in resolving project conflicts. **(4.0)**

11. Gave credit where credit was due. **(4.0)**

ASCE Looks to PMI for Leadership in Project Management – I recently ordered a project management book recommended in *ASCE News*. The book was entitled *Management by Projects* by Albert Hamilton. When I examined the book, I was delighted to find that the author has written two chapters around the PMBOK. PMI is clearly being recognized as a leader in project management even by the E/A industry! This means our competition will be using the knowledge provided by PMI–if they aren't already! –DEM

Qualities of Leadership by George P. Johnson

·**Integrity** – The crucial ingredient in any personal relationship is trust.

·**Discernment** – It combines perceptions and foresight with wisdom and judgment.

·**Passion** – The passion with which a leader holds on to core values and pursues a vision is contagious.

·**Empathy** – This is the quality that enables a leader to step beyond managing "human resources" to nourishing, motivating, and inspiring individuals.

·**Self-Confidence** – It is founded not on ego but on a clear understanding of personal strengths and weaknesses.

·**Humility** – The status of leader can never be achieved without convincing the led that they come first.

·**Caring** – The essence of leadership is convincing the led that you care deeply and would sacrifice your own self-interest for them.

·**Humor** – Leaders with a sense of humor take themselves less seriously, creating a relaxed atmosphere and promoting openness and candor.

"WHEN THE BEST LEADER'S WORK IS DONE THE PEOPLE SAY, "WE DID IT OURSELVES."
—LAO-TZU, CHINESE PHILOSOPHER

"LEADERSHIP IS THE MANAGER'S ABILITY TO GET SUBORDINATES TO DEVELOP THEIR CAPABILITIES BY INSPIRING THEM TO ACHIEVE." —JOHN REINECKE & WILLIAM SCHOELL

"A GREAT LEADER IS A PERSON WHO HAS THE ABILITY TO GET OTHER PEOPLE TO DO WHAT THEY DON'T WANT TO DO AND LIKE IT." —PRESIDENT HARRY TRUMAN

PROJECT MANAGEMENT EDUCATIONAL OPPORTUNITIES

The Business of Project Management – Session 2

·October 19 & 20, 1999 (Note this course has been changed to 2 days in lieu of 2.5 days)

·City Plaza Hotel, Iowa City

·Instructors – Conrad Baumler, Anne Cameron, Jim Cutler, Tom Hayden, Dale Moore, Steve Noack and Guy Patten (32 students are registered)

Project Management Basic Skills

·January 20 & 21, 2000

·Location to be determined

·Instructor – Jim Wansack. This course includes the basic skills of the PMBOK and the basic knowledge of our project management program. The course will be offered to those project managers who have not yet received the course and other selected individuals. *Stay tuned for more details!*

A LEADER OR A MANAGER?
continued from front cover

mismatch, you should correct that problem. No magic formula e> that will make a bad match more acceptable to the individual.

The best book on leadership that I know of is *The Leadership Cl lenge*, by Kouzes and Posner. Their point is that it isn't enough to kn how to apply the tools of project management. The tools are necess but are not sufficient for success. To be really effective, you need to a leader. Want a simple test of whether you're a leader? Just ask, ' I have followers?" That's the only test you will ever need.

JIM LEWIS, PH.D., IS EDITOR-IN-CHIEF OF THE *SUCCE FUL PROJECT MANAGEMENT* NEWSLETTER, AN EXPE ENCED PROJECT MANAGER, RENOWNED AUTHOR AND SPECTED EDUCATOR WHO TEACHES PROJECT MANA MENT THROUGHOUT THE WORLD. LEWIS IS THE AUTH OF *PROJECT PLANNING, SCHEDULING & CONTROL* THAT PART OF PMI'S "BOX" OF BOOKS. —DEM

SHIVE·HATTERY

WHAT DO CLIENTS AND TEAM MEMBERS EXPECT FROM PROJECT MANAGERS?

By Dale Moore

PROJECT MANAGERS OFTEN ASK, "WHAT DO I NEED TO DO TO PLEASE CLIENTS?" AND, "WHAT DO I NEED TO DO TO PLEASE PROJECT TEAM MEMBERS?" THE ANSWERS AREN'T EASY. IN FACT, THE SATISFACTION OF CLIENTS AND TEAM MEMBERS IS A COMPLEX ISSUE. HOWEVER, I SUGGEST THE FIRST PLACE TO LOOK FOR THE ANSWER IS IN THE CLIENT AND TEAM MEMBER SURVEYS. REVIEW THE SURVEY QUESTIONS LISTED BELOW AND DETERMINE HOW YOU CAN IMPROVE IN EACH OF THE AREAS INCLUDED IN THESE SURVEYS. FOCUSING ON THESE AREAS SHOULD RESULT IN SUBSTANTIAL IMPROVEMENT IN CLIENT AND TEAM MEMBER SATISFACTION. —DEM

Client Service Quality Questionnaire

*Company results through 8/31/99

(1=service did not meet the expectations   3=service was average 5=service exceeded expectations)

1. My expectations were met. **(4.2)**

2. I received value for the fees charged. **(4.1)**

3. Shive-Hattery met my schedule. **(4.2)**

4. Shive-Hattery worked within my budget. **(4.1)**

5. Shive-Hattery was responsive to my needs. **(4.4)**

6. I enjoyed working with Shive-Hattery's staff. **(4.6)**

7. Shive-Hattery addressed project conflict promptly and effectively. **(4.2)**

8. Change orders were not a problem. **(4.2)**

9. How would you rank Shive-Hattery compared to other design firms? **(4.1)**

Team Member Evaluation

*Company results through 8/31/99

(1=strongly disagree 2=disagree 3=generally agree 4=agree 5=strongly agree)

1. Clearly defined and communicated team member roles, responsibilities and accountabilities at the beginning of the project. **(3.9)**

2. Maintained a good relationship with the team members during the project. **(4.2)**

3. Was a good listener who actively sought team member ideas and solutions for how to deliver this project. **(4.1)**

4. Proactively developed and maintained backup strategies (contingency plans) in anticipation of potential project problems. **(3.7)**

5. Used a workable set of project planning, project re-planning and control tools. **(3.7)**

6. Continuously stressed to project team members the importance of meeting budget, schedule commitments and customer (internal and external) expectations. **(4.0)**

7. Was readily accessible to team members. **(4.0)**

8. Kept the project team informed in a timely manner. **(3.9)**

9. Was willing to help people realize their full potential; tried to bring out the best in people. **(4.0)**

10. Was timely and effective in resolving project conflicts. **(4.0)**

11. Gave credit where credit was due. **(4.0)**

ASCE Looks to PMI for Leadership in Project Management – I recently ordered a project management book recommended in *ASCE News*. The book was entitled *Management by Projects* by Albert Hamilton. When I examined the book, I was delighted to find that the author has written two chapters around the PMBOK. PMI is clearly being recognized as a leader in project management even by the E/A industry! This means our competition will be using the knowledge provided by PMI–if they aren't already! –DEM

Qualities of Leadership by George P. Johnson

·**Integrity** – The crucial ingredient in any personal relationship is trust.

·**Discernment** – It combines perceptions and foresight with wisdom and judgment.

·**Passion** – The passion with which a leader holds on to core values and pursues a vision is contagious.

·**Empathy** – This is the quality that enables a leader to step beyond managing "human resources" to nourishing, motivating, and inspiring individuals.

·**Self-Confidence** – It is founded not on ego but on a clear understanding of personal strengths and weaknesses.

·**Humility** – The status of leader can never be achieved without convincing the led that they come first.

·**Caring** – The essence of leadership is convincing the led that you care deeply and would sacrifice your own self-interest for them.

·**Humor** – Leaders with a sense of humor take themselves less seriously, creating a relaxed atmosphere and promoting openness and candor.

"WHEN THE BEST LEADER'S WORK IS DONE THE PEOPLE SAY, "WE DID IT OURSELVES."
–LAO-TZU, CHINESE PHILOSOPHER

"LEADERSHIP IS THE MANAGER'S ABILITY TO GET SUBORDINATES TO DEVELOP THEIR CAPABILITIES BY INSPIRING THEM TO ACHIEVE." –JOHN REINECKE & WILLIAM SCHOELL

"A GREAT LEADER IS A PERSON WHO HAS THE ABILITY TO GET OTHER PEOPLE TO DO WHAT THEY DON'T WANT TO DO AND LIKE IT." –PRESIDENT HARRY TRUMAN

PROJECT MANAGEMENT EDUCATIONAL OPPORTUNITIES

The Business of Project Management – Session 2

·October 19 & 20, 1999 (Note this course has been changed to 2 days in lieu of 2.5 days)

·City Plaza Hotel, Iowa City

·Instructors – Conrad Baumler, Anne Cameron, Jim Cutler, Tom Hayden, Dale Moore, Steve Noack and Guy Patten (32 students are registered)

Project Management Basic Skills

·January 20 & 21, 2000

·Location to be determined

·Instructor – Jim Wansack. This course includes the basic skills of the PMBOK and the basic knowledge of our project management program. The course will be offered to those project managers who have not yet received the course and other selected individuals. *Stay tuned for more details!*

A LEADER OR A MANAGER?
continued from front cover

mismatch, you should correct that problem. No magic formula ex that will make a bad match more acceptable to the individual.

The best book on leadership that I know of is *The Leadership Ch lenge*, by Kouzes and Posner. Their point is that it isn't enough to kr how to apply the tools of project management. The tools are necess but are not sufficient for success. To be really effective, you need to a leader. Want a simple test of whether you're a leader? Just ask, ' I have followers?" That's the only test you will ever need.

JIM LEWIS, PH.D., IS EDITOR-IN-CHIEF OF THE *SUCCE FUL PROJECT MANAGEMENT* NEWSLETTER, AN EXPE ENCED PROJECT MANAGER, RENOWNED AUTHOR AND SPECTED EDUCATOR WHO TEACHES PROJECT MANAC MENT THROUGHOUT THE WORLD. LEWIS IS THE AUTH OF *PROJECT PLANNING, SCHEDULING & CONTROL* THAT PART OF PMI'S "BOX" OF BOOKS. –DEM